Financially Single

Financial Advice for the Divorced or Widowed

By

Meredith Dekker & Dan Cuprill

Table of Contents

About Meredith Dekker

When I started my Financial Planning Business in 2002 it was not that I totally understood what a financial planner did.

I worked in the telecommunications industry at the time of a massive layoff. I did some consulting for the industry, but that can be a lonely place. I felt like I was at a pivotal milestone in my life. I was offered a couple of jobs but after talking to my nephew who was a financial planner, I decided to take the road less traveled. So, I turned down a sure thing and ventured off on my own. It was frightening but I did not let my fear drive the direction I wanted to go.

I was very blessed to have a mentor who had the same values I did and was able to help me understand what it meant to be a financial advisor. I wanted the relationship with the clients I was working with and to really understand what they were all about.

I am the youngest of six kids and I grew up in a small farming community in the Midwest. There is a fourteen-year span between my oldest sibling and myself. Until eleven I lived on a dairy farm.

Although my siblings did not think I had to do as much work as they did, I did do my fair share of chores. Moving into town was a big deal where my mother opened a fabric store and my father sold feed. My dad had a knack of drawing me into his stories of a difficult childhood and of fighting in WWII. He had landed on Omaha Beach on D-Day in the second wave, fought in the Battle of the Bulge and how he and his buddy took care of an orphan girl in France waiting to come home. I think that is part of the reason I love history and hearing everyone's stories.

I worked in one or both of those businesses until I went off to college. That education was so valuable and at the time I had no idea what I was learning. Growing up on a farm teaches you to think differently. The seed you plant in the spring takes months to mature and the same goes for relationships with your clients. It also taught me that you cannot live paycheck to paycheck. The money you get for your harvest needs to last through the winter and I know there were many times when my dad wondered if it would.

Even after I was married, I started my own little retail business selling sewing machines. I worked side by side with my husband in his trucking business and then when we moved to California, I began working in the medical field. Home computers were just coming on the market and I quickly learned how to put a PC together from someone in the office I worked in. I even had a "Prodigy" email address. Many of you have no idea what I am talking about, but it was one of the first email services offered by AT&T. I did not have anyone to email, but that changed very quickly. When my husband was asked to move to Arizona in 1993 to start a logistics branch for Toyota, we were ready to take on a new chapter in our lives.

When I am working with clients I love getting to know where they came from and what has been their journey because we all have an awesome story to tell. I love formulating the next steps for our clients.

One of the greatest compliments that I have ever received from one of my clients was when he told me "this is why we are here, because you can communicate with my wife and myself." The relationship with my client is first, everything else is secondary. Anyone who works with us can expect the same. We need to get to know you and understand your story before we can move forward to making a plan that fits your needs.

When I am not working, I love spending time with my husband, three married children, grandkids, sewing quilts and taking long hikes in the woods. Life goes by quickly and learning to appreciate each person I encounter has been an immeasurable blessing. I have had a diversified background and I feel very strongly that it has helped me to understand my clients and each person's unique situation. You can always sit in front of a computer, but until you have met with someone face to face to hear their story, you are missing a major component.

Introduction by Meredith Dekker

Many women who take the time to educate themselves about finances will search their libraries or purchase a Kindle book on finance. These are typically about making a budget, investing etc. But when you are suddenly a 50-year-old woman whose kids are all grown, and you find yourself either divorced or a widow you may need to find a unique financial perspective.

I have been working with divorced and widowed clients since I started my business in 2002. Even though it is financial planning, there are unique circumstances that need to be addressed.

You may have never handled your finances before. Perhaps you are uncertain about the risks of what you are getting yourself into. I want to assure you that I go by the old kindergarten philosophy that "there is no dumb question".

In this book you will learn how standing alone in the financial world does not mean you are standing lost in the world. Conventional financial planning needs may not fit your circumstances and this book will guide you make necessary changes if needed.

Imagine a financial advisor who only gave you the exact same advice that he has given to every one of his clients.

For instance, you could see young people advised to invest in bonds or others directed to make distributions in risky companies. That is an extreme example, but my point is, everyone is different, and each person has a unique situation.

As humans, we struggle with common sense. We are naturally wired to always avoid pain. This survival mechanism often makes doing the things the traditional way somewhat difficult.

I encourage you to keep an open mind. After each chapter we have provided additional reading on the topic.

If at any time you wish to discuss the topics in greater detail, call me at (480) 897-1067 or email Meredith.dekker@dekkerfinancial.com

--Meredith Dekker ChFC®, CDFA®

Where to Begin

By Meredith Dekker

When you are young and in love, seeing yourself as independently single again just does not cross your mind. What will your wedding day be like? How many children will you have? What career will you have? Those are the questions that are on your mind, but usually not "what if I am alone?"

I have seen the most intelligent, hard-working, wonderful women that have found themselves wondering why they had not been more prepared or aware. A person who is lost in the woods may be asking themselves the same questions.

It does not really matter if you ended up financially alone because you were divorced, widowed, or just choose to be alone; the financial questions may still look like a huge obstacle that needs to overcome.

The first thing I want you to know is that "There are no dumb questions!" So many of my clients are afraid to ask the questions they are unsure of. Many women have heard some of the terms of investing like, mutual fund, stocks, bonds, diversification, Dow Jones, S&P500, etc. But many have only a vague idea of what these terms mean. Believe me when I tell you, many men do not know either. You don't have to know everything. What's important is that you're looking to learn and improve.

I would love for every one of my clients to ask those questions that they feel so uncomfortable asking. Letting me know what you do and do not understand is one of the first things we need to clarify if we are going to work together. Acting like you know will only lead to more confusion and misunderstanding.

The second thing is to trust the person you are working with. If you do not feel comfortable or are not confident you are hearing the WHOLE story, and you have asked many times without any answers, it is time to move on.

The most difficult client to work with is one who does not trust me. Trust doesn't happen overnight, but when there's a lack of trust, it's important to acknowledge why. Sometimes it's a matter of proceeding slowly, and other times there are underlying issues that need to be addressed before any real progress can be made.

The third thing to know is that I am going to ask some questions that you may think do not pertain to the situation. Usually, it does!

I may ask you if you have a will or a trust. If you would like to change careers? What will your Social Security be? So many more, and each one has to do with the advice that I give you. Each person is different!

Fourth; the internet is not always correct, and your friends and family may not be either. I have had many clients come to me and say, "my brother told me to do this", etc. Unless that person is a fiduciary and a trained financial advisor, you may want to rethink taking their advice. I do not care how rich you think they are; every person is different, and they may not have all the facts to understand your financial situation.

One of the first things I tell my clients is to seek your family and friends for moral support and comfort, not for financial advice.

Do you recognize a theme here? Yes, it is the importance of asking questions! Questions will help you find the answers you need. There is not any book that can cover every topic and every issue, but if you feel comfortable enough to ask the questions you may find the answers which in turn can give you the financial clarity you seek.

What Issues Should You Consider?

By Meredith Dekker

Financial insecurity can be found by just putting yourself in a category and labeling yourself as a Divorcee or a widow. This does not define who you are. It simply means a life-changing event has occurred in your life.

Yes, there are different issues that need to be addressed in the beginning, but ultimately my goal is to help you have the confidence to make financial decisions that will benefit you in the long and short term. First let me address some of those differences. However, some of these do over-lap, so do not skip reading them.

In the event of a divorce or even contemplating a divorce here are some quick questions for you to think about and discuss with your financial advisor.

- Tax planning issues

- What tax filing status must you use? Your marital status on December 31st of the year you are divorced is the determining factor.
- Which child will you be claiming?
- Did your marriage last at least 10 years? If so, you may be eligible for Social Security benefits under your spouse's record after the divorce.
- Do you need to update your estate planning documents and beneficiary designations?
- Do you have dependent children who will likely go to college? Who is going to pay and if the school requires FAFSA information from the custodial parent, this may make a difference in the amount received?
- Do you need to adjust your cash flow needs?
- Is a plan needed to divide assets and liabilities and if so, has it been agreed upon and implemented?
- Do you have debts that you are unaware of? If you are unsure, check your credit report and monitor it on a regular basis.
- Do you have an emergency fund?

- Do retirement accounts need to be transferred?
- Do you know how to avoid a 10% penalty in the event you only receive retirement assets but are not 59 ½?
- What is your housing situation? Do you need to sell your home? If you intend to sell within two years of divorce you can take advantage of the marital exclusion, which is $500,000.00. If you wait longer that will be reduced to a single status exclusion which is $250,000.00.
- Have you been insured under your husband's health insurance?
- If your spouse was a business owner, was there a plan set up in the event of divorce?

In the event of your spouse dying prematurely, you are going to have to address many of those same issues. However, I will list a few additional ones here.

- Tax planning issues
  - If you filed as married filing jointly you can continue to file as MFJ in the year your spouse passed away.

- o Was your spouse receiving a required minimum distribution? If so, you will need to satisfy that amount on behalf of your spouse before the end of the year.
- Did your marriage last at least 9 months? If so, you may be eligible for Social Security benefits under your spouse's record or survivorship benefits.
- Do you need to update your estate planning documents and beneficiary designations?
- Do you have dependent children? They are entitled to Social Security Benefits until the age of 18.
- Do you need to adjust your cash flow needs?
- Do you have debts that you are unaware of? If you are unsure, check your credit report and monitor it on a regular basis.
- Do you have an emergency fund?
- Do retirement accounts need to be transferred to your name?
- What is your housing situation? Do you need to sell your home? If you intend to sell within two years of your spouse's death and other conditions are met, you can take

advantage of the marital exclusion, which is $500,000.00. If you wait longer that will be reduced to a single status exclusion which is $250,000.00.

- Have you been insured under your husband's health insurance?
- If your husband was still employed, did he have stock options, grants, or restricted stock units? If so, you may be entitled to those.
- If your spouse was a business owner, was there a plan set up in the event of his premature death?

As you can see, there are many situations that overlap and apply to you if you are divorcing or widowed. These are only a few items but consider these questions when talking to your qualified financial advisor.

There Is No Nostradamus

By Dan Cuprill & Meredith Dekker

"Uncertainty is the only certainty there is and knowing how to live with insecurity is the only security." *--John Allen Paulos*

Do not go looking up Nostradamus, it may be a little depressing.

Imagine a TV network dedicated to fortune telling. Every day, it features highly educated people who strongly believe they can predict the future. Like Isaiah, they offer their prophecy for free. Unlike Isaiah, these seers are wrong about 80% of the time. Yet, despite the failures, viewers continue to watch. Even worse, many stake their entire personal fortunes on the advice.

Would you watch such a network? Millions do. In fact, there is not just one such channel, but many.

Go ahead...turn on a business channel, especially around noon on a weekday. These channels bring on one market "expert" after another to give out stock tips or some insight as to where the market is headed.

Here is a little reality: No one...and we mean no one...knows where investment markets are headed in the next week, month, or year. If they did know, they certainly would not tell you for free. In fact, they would not tell you at all because such information would be far too valuable to even sell.

Remember the rule of transitive properties from Ms. Cheeseman's math class (more on her in a minute). If A is greater than B...and B is greater than C, then A is also greater than C.   Or to put it another way, if Bill is taller than Mike, and Mike is taller than Jim, then Bill is also taller than Jim. Got it?

Okay...now pay very close attention.

Markets react to news. Do you agree? Every time stocks drop in price, isn't there always some news event attributed to it. (9/11, Microsoft anti-trust suit, the Fed raising interest rates, earnings reports lower than expected)?

News is unpredictable. Do you agree?   Did you know any of the following events would happen before they occurred?

1. Hijacked airplanes crashing into the World Trade Center and the Pentagon.
2. The Kennedy Assassination.
3. The announcement of Toxic Asset Relief Program.
4. Arthur Anderson's false accounting of Enron.
5. Pearl Harbor (okay...this one isn't fair. You probably weren't alive).
6. A Pandemic called Covid-19.

In response to each of these news events, equity markets dropped rapidly. If you did know about these events a week before they occurred, you could have made billions of dollars.

Two movies come to mind that demonstrate this reality.

<u>Casino Royale (2006):</u> James Bond seeks to defeat a card playing terrorist who makes huge rates of return by shorting stocks on companies and then staging acts of sabotage on those corporations because he knows it will drive down their stock price. In other words, he knows the news before anyone else because he's creating it.

<u>Wall Street (1987):</u> Gordon Gekko hires aspiring trader Bud Fox to "stop sending me information and start bringing me some." So, Bud breaks into offices at night, spies on company executives, and relays insider information told to him by his father. As a result, Gekko has "news" that no one else has, allowing him to trade ahead of the market.

So, if news is unpredictable and market performance reacts to news, then market performance is unpredictable.

Wait a minute. Are you saying then that all those Wall Street experts like Jim Cramer and Charles Paine really have no idea what they are talking about?

Yes...and No. They certainly know many things. But so do millions of other traders. Everything they know is already factored into a stock's price. It is what they do not know, the future news, which will drive stock prices. They are simply speculating as to what they think the news will be.

Sometimes they get it right...most of the time they get it wrong. Studies show that on average 80% of all professional portfolio managers fail to beat their benchmark index. Of the 20% who do, there are very few repeaters.

The Law of Large Numbers

Do you remember taking statistics in college? I do, rolling that dice for hours was mind numbing.

Imagine we fill the New Orleans Super Dome with 35,000 people. On the PA system, we instruct them all to stand up and remove a quarter from their pocket.

On our mark, they all flip the coin. Those who flipped heads (about 17,500) remain standing. Those who flipped tails sit down. We now repeat this exercise, again and again. With 35,000 people flipping coins, we are willing to bet our houses that at least one person in the dome will flip heads ten straight times. In fact, we would not be surprised if at least 20 people did it.

The law of large numbers states that if you have enough people try to do something, someone will succeed regardless of skill level. The individual who tossed heads 10 straight times...is he an expert coin flipper? Does he somehow understand the gravitational properties between his quarter, his wrist, and the earth? Or was he just lucky?

Guess how many professional portfolio managers exist today? Yup...about 35,000. Over 2,000 work for Fidelity alone. Someone is bound to speculate correctly on the market's reaction to news that has yet to occur.

In fact, the one person at Fidelity who predicted the down market of 2008 was promoted in her job.

The successful coin flipper is called lucky. The successful stock picker is called a guru and gets his face on magazines.

Again, we will concede that these people are smart. Most went to the very best business schools in the country where they were taught that markets and stock prices are not predictable. But when they arrived on Wall Street, they were told how their firms really make money: trades.

Over 1 billion trades a month at $9 per trade on the New York Stock Exchange alone. You do the math. It is in *their* best interest to trade...not yours.

We do think that these very smart people honestly believe they have found a peek into the future. If there were only a handful of them researching companies, then they might be onto something. But there are thousands, all crunching the same data. Furthermore, their efforts to buy and sell ahead of the market incur costs that lower their rates of return.

In 2013, Eugene Fama won the Nobel Prize in economics for stating in the 1960's that something is worth only what someone is willing to pay for it. (That is exactly what my dad always said when my mom wanted to save something and he wanted to throw it away: "It's not worth anything until you find someone to buy it, then it's worth only what they paid for it") Called "The Efficient Market Hypothesis", Fama showed (with a bunch of math) that the current price of a stock or bond is the correct price. Nothing is overvalued or undervalued until someone offers or agrees to a different price.

If you buy a house for $300,000, spend $50,000 for improvement, and put it up for sale, how much is it worth if the highest offer you receive is $290,000?

Correct. It is worth $290,000.

So, if it is true for real estate, why not stocks?

The $6 Watch

Zach Norris is a young man with a passion for fine watches. Understanding that often people do not know the value of their old jewelry, he routinely visits thrift shops and garage sales looking for great deals. If he sees a watch that he knows he can quickly resell for a profit, he will buy it for the asking price and then quickly find a new buyer. In January of 2015, he bought a $6 watch at his local Goodwill store and then sold it for $35,000.

Norris is to watches what Wall Street portfolio managers aspire to be to stocks. But unlike Mr. Norris, they deal in public information. Had Goodwill known the watch was worth $35,000, would they have sold it for $6? Or would the prior owner have given away the watch to Goodwill in the first place? Of course not. Mr. Norris had insider knowledge. In this case, he can legally act on it. But in the world of security trading, such a move can land you in jail (see Martha Stewart and Bud Fox).

Perhaps there was a time when news traveled slowly enough for someone to get a jump. Those days are over.

There is no Nostradamus. News occurs randomly, and so too will stock and bond prices. All we have going for us is that over the history of mankind, good news has outperformed bad. Despite world wars, famines, epidemics, assassinations, national debt, and disco, capitalism finds a way to improve the quality of life. The quality of your life today dwarfs that of every king and queen of the middle ages. It dwarfs that of your great grandparents, and even your grandparents. Is it not only logical to assume that in the future we will witness massive amounts of bad news but overall, we will prosper?

Hence, actions like market timing and stock picking are far less likely to succeed than buying, holding, and rebalancing a broadly diversified portfolio.

Don't just take our word for it (books to read)

The Investment Answer by Daniel Goldie and Gordon Murray
Random Walk Down Wall Street by Burton Malkeil
The Smartest Investment Book You'll Ever Own by Dan Solin
What Wall Street Doesn't Want You to Know by Larry Swedroe
Winning the Loser's Game by Charles Ellis

Your Math Teacher Was Right (but you always knew that).

By Dan Cuprill & Meredith Dekker

"Mathematics are well and good, but nature keeps dragging us around by the nose. "–Albert Einstein

You remember Ms. Cheeseman...the matronly math teacher who has been teaching out of the same book for thirty years because "the math hasn't changed. As you looked at the inside cover of the book, you saw the names and years of the prior holders. "Was it as boring for Fred Saddlemire in 1968 as it is for me now?" you asked yourself. "Was Ms. Cheeseman ever cool?" "Only the time she got caught kissing the English teacher in the classroom".

The one question that rose above all others was, "Will I ever need to know this stuff?"

Ms. Cheeseman assured us we would. Now you are about to see that she was right.

Meet Hans & Franz. When not pumping iron and injecting themselves with steroids, they are drawing income from their savings accumulated from years on late night TV. Aside from an occasional State Farm commercial, the two are pretty much retired.

Convinced that no one should invest like a girlie man, Hans has invested heavily in equities under the belief that over time he stands to earn a higher rate of return. Chances are he will be right.

Franz is no stranger to machismo but opts for a portfolio that is likely to produce a lower, more consistent rate of return. Starting with one million each, they both desire to withdraw $50,000 per year to supplement their SNL royalty checks.

Hans and Franz are about to learn what Ms. Cheeseman taught us years ago:

Average may not be as important as consistency of return.

Hans: $1,000,000			
Year	Withdrawal	Return	Y/E Value
1	$50,000.00	-13	$826,500.00
2	$50,000.00	-20%	$661,200.00
3	$50,000.00	5%	$694,260.00
4	$50,000.00	-7%	$599,161.80
5	$50,000.00	20%	$658,994.16
6	$50,000.00	25%	$761,242.70
7	$50,000.00	-25%	$533,432.03
8	$50,000.00	45%	$700,976.44
9	$50,000.00	30%	$846,269.37
10	$50,000.00	20%	***$908,060.56***
Return Average: 8%			

Franz: $1,000,000			
Year	Withdrawal	Return	Y/E Value
1	$50,000.00	6%	$1,007,000.00
2	$50,000.00	8%	$1,087,560.00
3	$50,000.00	7%	$1,163,689.20
4	$50,000.00	11%	$1,236,195.01
5	$50,000.00	-4%	$1,138,747.21
6	$50,000.00	6%	$1,154,072.04
7	$50,000.00	12%	$1,236,560.69
8	$50,000.00	-2%	$1,162,829.48
9	$50,000.00	10%	$1,224,112.42
10	$50,000.00	6%	***$1,244,559.17***
Return Average: 6%			

As you can see, although Hans indeed earned a higher average return (8% vs. 6%) at the end of ten years, he has considerably less money than his body-building brother. Why? Every year, the two sell a part of their portfolios' shares to generate cash. When shares rise in value, it requires fewer shares to generate $50,000. When share prices fall, Hans must sell more. Those extra shares, once sold, are gone. It matters not what his portfolio does in the future in relation to those shares. He will never get them back.

By minimizing his potential downside, Franz has more money even though he averaged less over time. Fewer negative years means he sells fewer shares.

This phenomenon exists only because Hans and Franz need to sell shares for cash. Had they never needed to sell shares, then Hans would have more much money than Franz, despite the volatility. This is the <u>Math of Retirement.</u>

Ms. Cheeseman taught us that nothing in life performs consistently--not the weather, not your golf score, and certainly not an investment portfolio. This lack of consistency can be measured. It is called standard deviation. The lower the standard deviation, the more likely you will earn the average return each year. So, if you found a portfolio with a guaranteed return of 8% every year, then the standard deviation would be zero. Good luck finding that. Chances are that the best you'll do in seeking your 8% is a portfolio with a standard deviation of ten. So, what does that mean?

> **If Average Return is 8% and Standard Deviation is ten, then:**
>
> 66% of the time: You will have a one-year return between -2% and 18%.
>
> 95% of the time: You will have a one-year return between -12% and 28%.
>
> 99% of the time: You will have a one-year return between -22% and 38%.

If you are an investor, then your portfolio also has a long-term average return and a standard deviation to go along with it. The problem is that very few people know this, nor do they understand the "normal" volatility that comes with it. If they did, we think they would be much less likely to panic.

For example, if a portfolio has the dimensions described in the chart above, should we be surprised (or even disappointed) if we earn a return of -6% each year?

Of course not. We already know going in, that this is very likely. We also know that over time, it is more likely that we'll have more positive results than negative results. Guaranteed? No. Likely? Yes.

Think of it like baking a cake. You can put in the best ingredients, but you have soup unless you put the cake in the oven for the right amount of time.

Results do not come in a linear fashion, no matter how badly we wish they did. What in life does? Do the giant redwoods of northern California grow the same number of feet every year? Does it take you the same number of minutes to drive to work each day? Do farmers dig up their corn seeds every few days to see if they are sprouting, or have they learned to trust the process?

It is essential that you know the long-term average return and standard deviation of your portfolio allocation. Without knowing, you are simply winging it; and your survival mechanism stands a much better chance of over-riding your logic.

Know your math. Make Ms. Cheeseman proud!

Don't just take our word for it (books to read):
The Intelligent Asset Allocator by William Bernstein
All About Asset Allocation by Richard Feri
Asset Allocation by Roger Gibson

The Boogeyman is Real
By Dan Cuprill & Meredith Dekker

"The only two things that scare me are God and the IRS" –Dr. Dre

Assuming that you do not define patriotism by the amount you pay in tax, what follows should be useful.

If you are one of the 53% of Americans who pay federal income taxes, then it is likely you pay more than what is legally required. If you own a small business, then it's almost a sure thing that you are overpaying And if you are single you are paying more than a couple. This puts you in a unique box which begins to snowball the older you are.

The Seven Most Expensive Words in the English Language: My CPA takes care of my taxes.

From our experience, most CPAs do a great job of filing taxes; but very few actually do any tax real planning. When I ask people, when was the last time their CPA said he found a way to lower your taxes by $4,000, they usually give me a blank stare and then say, "Never."

Does your CPA/Tax Preparer ever:

- Call you with proactive strategies to achieve a tax-free retirement?

- Demonstrate how to restructure your 401k/403b/IRA accounts to avoid future taxation?

- How to collect your social security benefits TAX FREE?

- Show you how to structure your business to minimize employment taxes?

- Show you how you can hire children (or grandchildren) to shift income from yourself to them?

- Help you choose the right retirement plan for your business?

- Explain how each of your investments is taxed and make suggestions on how to reduce it?

- Advise you on how to carefully consider which investments belong in taxable accounts and which investments belong in tax-advantaged accounts?

- Develop a plan for maximizing the value of any long-term capital loss carryforwards?

- Explain the rules governing "passive" income and losses and have a plan to avoid "suspended" losses?

- Meet with you throughout the year to discuss your business--or does he/she just wait until taxes are due?

- Give you a plan for minimizing taxes--or does he/she just wing it every year?

Aside from investing behavior, income taxes are the greatest obstacle to most investors. There is never an age at which you stop paying them. You paid tax on your social security as you put money into the system, and you will likely pay tax on the money as it comes out.

When you reach age 72, you must start paying tax on your retirement plans (401k, IRA, 403b). When you die, your heirs must also pay tax on whatever is left.

Your estate may be taxed again for simply being too big.

The code is, by design, very complicated. Too often, people just go along with it, unaware of the steps that can legally reduce their federal and state income taxes. This is especially important during retirement.

You have a choice of paying taxes now...or later. To many, procrastination seems logical when it comes paying the IRS. For years people have socked away massive amounts of money in 401ks, 403bs, IRAs. The idea is you invest it now in a tax-deductible account while you are in a high tax bracket. Then you withdraw it at a lower tax bracket when you retire. Or so you hope.

What if taxes rise in the future? The US owes over $20 trillion. Projections suggest this amount will continue to rise as more and more baby boomers retire and more stimulus packages are passed in legislation. This translates into Fewer people paying taxes and more requiring things like Medicare, Medicaid, and Social Security. From where will that money come?

Case Study

Karen Tucker is 65 years old, previously divorced, remarried and now a widow. Her investment accounts consist of her IRA and her deceased husband's rollover IRA which is worth $600,000. Karen collects $2,200 a month from social security, which is based on her previous husbands' earnings. Karen has elected to wait until the age of 70 for her to have the maximum benefit of her own Social Security.

She needs $7,000 a month to live comfortably, so she withdraws $4,800 a month from her retirement accounts.
To determine how much of her social security check is subject to taxation, we add the IRA withdrawals ($57,600) to one-half of the social security payments ($13,200.00)

This gives them a modified adjust gross income (MAGI) of $70,800.00. Whenever the MAGI exceeds $34,000 for a single person or qualifying widow, then up to 85% of their check is subjected to taxation.

Compare those numbers to a married couple and additional Social Security from a spouse. The additional income of $1,800 from Social Security would mean less money would come from the IRA account and a MAGI would be $43,000 instead of the lower amount. You can see as a single filer you are at a greater disadvantage and will pay more in taxes and deplete your savings at a faster rate than a married couple.

Assuming she files as single and uses the standard deduction, Karen owes $15,576.00 in taxes verses a married couple who would only be paying $4,300 in Federal income taxes.

Now, what if she had decided a few years back to convert her rollover IRAs to a Roth IRA? Doing so would have triggered tax at the time of conversion, but no tax will ever be owned on the accounts again. Depending on her income at the time of conversion she may only pay 10% of taxes on that IRA money. Even if their accounts double in value, there is no tax associated with a Roth withdrawal. Not only is there no tax on Roth IRA withdrawals, but now there would also be no tax owed on their Social Security benefits. Furthermore, Karen could now withdraw a lesser amount from her Roth IRA and therefore having her assets last for a longer period of time.

Imagine if federal income tax rates double in the future. By converting to a Roth, Karen has added another layer of protection herself.

Another tax advantaged vehicle is permanent life insurance. Money in the policy grows tax deferred and can be accessed tax free via a policy loan. While buying life insurance may not be an appropriate vehicle for Karen at this time, she may be able to utilize such a tool. This feature is a great reason to keep your policy even after you have stopped working.

Like a lot of people we meet, Karen relied solely on her accountant for tax advice. But from our experience, many accountants work as tax filers, not tax planners.

The timing of the conversion is critical and must be a part of the financial plan which includes the tax planning.

Tax planning is one of the most ignored areas of financial planning, and failure to address IRS lien on savings is ruining people. It is not the job of the IRS to tell you how to lower your taxes. It is your job. If you do not know how, you need to find a professional who does. You will not find him/her inside a box of turbo tax software.

The tax code is very complicated. Too often people just go along with it, unaware of the steps that can legally reduce their federal and state income taxes. Failure to address this issue can mean you are not worth anywhere close to what you think.

Don't just take our word for it (books to read):
How to Pay Zero Taxes by J.K. Lasser
How to Defuse the Ticking Tax Time Bomb by Dan Cuprill

It Will Probably End Badly
By Dan Cuprill & Meredith Dekker

"It's paradoxical, that the idea of living a long life appeals to everyone, but the idea of getting old doesn't appeal to anyone." – Andy Rooney

The first chapter ended with a statement that the future is always likely to be better than the past. For society as a whole, we truly believe that. As for our individual lives, we know that life is finite. The Grim Reaper is undefeated. And while modern medicine has made huge strides in fighting heart disease, diabetes, and cancer, we all still die.

If you are a widow or widower, you know that life can be sniffed out quickly or drawn out through a long illness.. Here today living life to the fullest...gone tomorrow.

As a society, we are living longer and as a woman we statistically living longer. That is a good thing, but that also means our money must last longer. It means that eventually we will become weak and likely to need help with those things we only want to do for ourselves (custodial care).

Some stats from the National Institute for Health:

- If you reach age 65, there is a 70% chance you'll need custodial care.
- The average nursing home stay is almost three years.
- The average nursing home cost in Arizona is $96,000 a year.
- Nursing home costs rise at twice the average inflation rate.
- Medicare does not pay for Long Term Care.
- Medicaid is available only after you have spent down your assets.
- Most people in nursing homes are on Medicaid, but they did not start there.

Basically, you have three options when it comes to long term care.

- First, you can self-insure the exposure. Perhaps you have enough money to do just that. Remember...it's $96,000.000 a year now. At 6% inflation, the price will double in twelve years.

- Second, you cannot rely on Medicaid. Why not? Most do, but that's available only after you've spent down your own money. There are specific income standards, and they vary from state to state. Besides your income, your assets will be counted towards meeting eligibility requirements. A single person in Arizona can have a monthly income up to only $2,313 in 2019. If you are married it is $4,626. If you are single you can only have up to $2,000 in assets with a few allowable exclusions. You do not have to sell your house, but the government may attach a lien to it after you die so that it can recoup the cost of your care.
- Third, you can buy long term care insurance. For many people, this is the right choice. Often, we hear people say they will not buy it out of fear they'll never use it, and thus waste their money. We are going to let you in on a little secret: the people who go to

nursing homes with long term care do not win the game. It is those who have long term care insurance but die peacefully in their sleep, healthy today...dead tomorrow, who win the game.

When your car isn't stolen, do you regret owing auto insurance? Never feel regret for being prudent.

Long term care insurance can be expensive, but a few things can be done to reduce it:

1. Limit coverage to four years. Odds are very high you won't need the policy after four years. By limiting coverage to four years, you reduce the cost dramatically over a lifetime benefit policy.

2. Self-insure a part of the cost. If nursing homes in your area cost $200 per day, consider coverage for $150. Be sure to study the long-term impact of not being fully insured.

3. Take advantage of the "partnership" program that is available in some states. This allows you to exclude from your assets the total amount of Long-Term Care benefits you purchase. For example, you purchase a Long-term Care policy that will pay a maximum of $350,000. If you use all of your benefits, you can go on Medicare even if you have $350,000 left in your accounts.

4. There are ways to lower your costs also by combining Life Insurance with your long-term care. You can take the benefit as long-term care or a death benefit.

Whatever you do...have a plan! It's not a matter of if, but when!

Don't just take our word for it (a book to read):
Long Term Care: <u>Your Financial Planning Guide</u> by Phyllis Shelton

Your Brain is Messed Up
By Dan Cuprill & Meredith Dekker

"We have seen the enemy, and he is us."—Pogo

Perhaps the biggest obstacle (no, not *perhaps*...it really *is* the biggest) toward financial success is our own brain...our humanness...our emotions.

God gave us many gifts; but if misused, they can be self-destructive.

Consider weight loss. Technically, losing weight is very easy. We simply exercise more and eat less. Yet, we are the fattest nation on earth; and weight loss is a multi-billion-dollar industry. Why?

Investing is also quite simple: buy when prices are low. Sell when they are high. According to the Dalbar study, we see that simple strategy ignored all the time. People often do the complete opposite.

Let's take Marty McFly's time traveling Delorean back a few years....to 10,000 BC.

Meet your great, great, great, great, great, great, great, great, great (you get the idea) grandfather. We'll call him Fred. He lives in a cave with his mate Wilma and their children Pebbles and Bam Bam (whom they adopted after a T-Rex ate Barney & Betty Rubble).

Life is very simple for Fred and Wilma. Fred wakes up, sharpens his spear, and kills whatever he can find. He brings it back to the cave where Wilma cooks it.

Fred is motivated to stop the pains of hunger, cold, and predators. He seeks warmth and comfort where he can; but above all else, he tries to avoid pain for his family and himself. He does not know it, but Fred has within his brain a survival mechanism that motivates him to behave this way. It is his natural tendency to flee from danger. In fact, all animals have it--another gift from God. Fred does not worry about his cholesterol level, his A1C results, or his blood pressure. He merely wants to stay fed, warm, and safe. Fred was the original "couch potato" whenever the opportunity presented itself.

Food, water, safety, and warmth...that is all he thinks about. Morality, personal fulfillment, spirituality…. these do not matter to him at all. It is a struggle just to meet the basics.

Fast forward to present day. We do not have Fred's worries. Far from it. Food? In the US, a major health problem amongst our poor is obesity. Water, warmth…readily available. The survival mechanism that kept Fred alive until a sabretooth tiger ate him is still present in our brains. We do not use it often, but it's there…lurking.

Need to lose weight by eating less (painful) and exercising (even more painful). Forget it. Our brain tells us we are crazy. Stay in bed. Rest. Relax.

Fred did not care if he lived past age 40, but you do. Rather than helping you though, the survival mechanism is betraying you.

When your stocks fall in value, you experience pain. Your brain tells you that you must do something. You must sell. When what you sold starts increasing in value, you feel worse! You know logically that stocks are likely to rebound, but your brain convinces you that "this time is different."

While the survival mechanism is the worse feature of our psyche when it comes to investing, there are a few others that can be equally destructive:

Herding: When we were teenaged, we called it "peer pressure". Our mothers asked, "If Johnny told you to jump off a bridge, would you?" Hey, bridge jumping can be great fun.

When Frank in accounting tells you that everyone is dumping the index fund in the company 401k and loading up heavily on company stock, you need to remind yourself of something. Unless Frank is having secret meetings with the company chairman, he knows nothing more than the rest of the world. All the information about your company is already factored into its stock. Frank is just speculating. Sadly, there were several "Franks" working at Enron.

Confirmation Bias: We would all like to believe that we are objective thinkers, weighing all facts before making a decision or establishing a belief. Sorry...not true. There are things we WANT to believe are true. So much so, we will ignore any evidence to the contrary. Take Nikki's daughter, Georgie. At age 8, she is committed to believing in Santa Clause. She is heard from classmates that

St. Nick isn't real, but every year she finds evidence to the contrary (thanks to her mom). In her mind, the kids who do not believe are simply the ones who misbehave and receive nothing on December 25th.

For other people, we see confirmation bias in areas like climate change, the Kennedy assassination, or the future price of gold.

In 2001, Dan met a GE engineer who said he had no intention of ever diversifying away from his company stock. "I don't want to hear it," he said to us when we suggested a broader allocation. He was 64, and the stock comprised 100% of his portfolio. In the previous ten years, his net worth had tripled. It seemed invincible.

At that point, the stock was trading at $65 a share. Seven years later, it was worth $8.

When it comes to matters of finance, confirmation bias can be expensive.

Anchoring: Back to our GE engineer. His wife saw the potential mistake of holding just one stock, but even she could not be swayed toward logic because they knew diversification would trigger taxation. So anchored was she in her belief that taxes are bad, that she put herself in a position of eventually owing no tax because they lost most of their portfolio in 2008. Oh, to have Marty's DeLorean.

A successful investor understands that logic does not come naturally. He seeks out ways to ensure that when it comes to money, the left side of his brain stays in control.

Don't just take our word for it (books to read):
Predictably Irrational by Dan Ariely
The Behavior Gap by Carl Richards

Rick Perry Was Right.

By Dan Cuprill & Meredith Dekker

"The real sin with Social Security is that it's a long-term rip-off and a short-term scam."—Tony Snow

A Ponzi scheme is an investment fraud that involves the payment of purported returns to existing investors from funds contributed by new investors. Ponzi scheme organizers often solicit new investors by promising to invest funds in opportunities claimed to generate high returns with little or no risk.

In many Ponzi schemes, the fraudsters focus on attracting new money to make promised payments to earlier-stage investors to create the false appearance that investors are profiting from a legitimate business.

With little or no legitimate earnings, Ponzi schemes require a consistent flow of money from new investors to continue. Ponzi schemes tend to collapse when it becomes difficult to recruit new investors or when a large number of investors ask to cash out.

--United States Securities & Exchange Commission

In the 2012 election primary, pundits attacked Texas Governor Rick Perry for correctly describing the Social Security system as a Ponzi scheme. The system, which began in 1937, then taxed **Thirty-**

seven workers for every retiree a maximum total of $30 per year. Today, it taxes **three** workers for every retiree 6.2% of their earnings (up to $142,800 (2021)). If you are self-employed, you could pay the tax twice if you do not plan.

Money is taken from workers and is transferred to retirees. The rate of return is not guaranteed. Most people will average between two and four percent. Many will lose money if they die before they receive benefits equal to their contributions. Unlike your savings, you cannot leave your social security benefits to your children. At least Charles Ponzi gave some investors a high rate of return.

Social Security today is not what it was intended to be when President Roosevelt signed the program into existence in 1935. Its original intent was to aid Americans who could not take care of themselves, such as widows and orphans. It was never designed to be the sole means for retirement income, which it has become for many Americans today.

In 1935, life expectancy was 58; while the earliest one could collect benefits back then was age 65. On average, you were more likely to die than receive benefits. Ironically, the very first person to receive a check, Ida May Fuller, lived to be 100 years old. These days about 58 million people receive benefits.

Benefit Timing

For many retirees, the question of when to take benefits can be a difficult one. The longer you wait to start collecting, the larger your monthly check. Full retirement age is between 62 and 67 depending on what year you were born.

You can take benefits as early as 62 but receive 25% less per month than if you hold out until your full retirement age. If you wait until age 70 to collect, then you get 32% more. In real dollars that means if your full retirement benefit is $2,000 but you elected to take it at 62, you will receive $1,500 each month. Likewise, if you wait until age 70, you will receive $2,700 every month.

Life expectancy plays a major role in determining the timing of your social security benefits. The breakeven point for taking benefits at 62 vs. 70 is age 78.

If you had that time machine and knew your expiration date – no problem. Of course, if you delay taking your benefit, it may mean you have to spend more of your savings in the early years of retirement.

Many factors need to be taken into consideration when taking social security. For a free Social Security timing report, visit website, www.SSA.gov

What is the future of Social Security? Is it sustainable? What was once a 1% tax is now 6.2%. As fewer people pay in and more are recipients, the percentage could always be increased. The amount of income subject to the tax could be increased, and inflationary increases could be eliminated or decreased. Lots of appealing options...

No political party wants to broach the elimination of Social Security, and they likely will not. Social Security in its current state is not at all what Roosevelt had in mind in 1935, so change is always a strong possibility.

Don't Just Take Our Word For It (a book to read):
Get What's Yours: The Secrets to Maxing Out Your Social Security by Laurence J. Kotlikoff, Phillip Moeller and Paul Solman

---

Flat Abs, A Low A1C, And Wealth: To Get These, You Probably Need Help.

"The power of coaching is this - you are expected to give people the path to find answers, not the answers" --Tom Mahalo

At age 51, he finally got the news: "Dan, you are fat, your blood sugar is too high, and so is your blood pressure. Other than that, you're doing great...for a 70-year-old."

He could not argue with the doctor. Everything he said was true.

"If you're serious about this, I can coach you through it," he said. "Every three months, going forward, you'll come in for new blood work and a review of your eating habits for the past three months. In addition, you will spend time with my nutritionist. Lastly, you will hire a personal trainer who will give you a full body workout three times a week."

Three months later, Dan lost 15 pounds, and his blood sugar level (A1C) dropped from 7.1 to 5.7 (you want it below 6.5).

Could he have done it without the nutritionist and trainer? Technically, yes. Realistically, not a chance. When the alarm goes off at 5:30 a.m., he now jumps out of bed because the trainer awaits him at the gym. If it were up to Dan to work out alone, that alarm would never be set. He admits he would just procrastinate. When he did get around to exercising, it would be with half the intensity his trainer demands. Why? Because exercise is painful. Sleep is pleasurable. Steel cut oatmeal doesn't taste nearly as good as a Dunkin' Donut.

On our own, we rarely perform at our optimal level. A good coach will not only help achieve excellence; he'll assist in keeping us there. A good coach sees things we cannot (or don't want to see). He forces us to leave our comfort zone and to apply logic when emotion is in overdrive. He holds us accountable to ourselves.

One of the biggest failings in the financial services industry is the failure to understand this. The industry is dominated not by coaches (or even advisors) but by commission salesmen. They push product as the answer and then go looking for the question. Objectivity is lost, and the client pays the price.

A good wealth coach services his/her client with a holistic approach and commits himself/herself to putting the needs of the client first. This is called a financial fiduciary.

Over 20 years, we have refined our process to offer such a service. It is a four-step financial planning process called "Wise Women Wealth".

Step One: The Consultation-- We begin every first meeting with a simple question: "What will make this a great meeting for you today?" We want the client to set the agenda. More importantly, we want to know what keeps them up at night.

If on a scale of one to ten (ten means you sleep like a Rip Van Winkle, and one means you do not sleep at all), how do you rate your financial situation? If you are a nine or a ten, you're done. Give this book to a friend and go live your life. No need for any coaching, you are Laurene Powell Jobs, the widow of Apple co-founder Steve Jobs.

But if you are more like a seven (or lower), then what must occur for you to be a ten, aside from winning the lottery? We find that it is rarely about the amount of money one has. The most anxious people we have ever met had significant wealth. Despite that, they were fearful, frustrated, and even angry. In some cases, they were victimized by other advisors. To get most people to a ten, it takes a strategy that they have a hand in designing. They require a plan that details fully the pros and cons and is simple enough that they can explain it to a friend.

Do you need to be a financial expert to be a ten? No. Just like we do not need to know how a hybrid engine works to drive a car. We do need to know how to start the car. We need to know how to put the car in gear, and how to turn the wheel. We need to know when to add gas (unless it's a diesel), when to rotate the tires, and when to change the oil. Simple stuff, but it is required.

A well-designed financial strategy answers questions like:

1. How much can I spend during retirement without a strong chance of going broke?

2. What rate of return do I really need on my money, and how can I get it with the least amount of volatility?

3. How can I protect myself from speculation (stock picking, market timing)?

4. How will I deal with catastrophe, such as failing health?

5. How can I legally pay the IRS less?

6. How can I most efficiently transfer my assets at death?

Step Two: The Creation-- Then questions to step one are answered by making you part of the plan's design. A good coach listens to what you want to accomplish. Maybe it is to spend more time with children or grandchildren, buy a second home, travel the world. All those things take money. It is not that money is the end game it is what can you do with that money and how much do you need to make those dreams happen. There is a road map that needs to be drawn up and then decide what roads you want to take and then offer the pros and cons of achieving that goal. And trust me...there are always cons. Lots of them. You need to know them.

Together we draw up the map. How much of your income do you want guaranteed? Before you say, "all of it," know that guaranteed usually comes with two costs: low return and less for your heirs.

If you choose to have some or all your money in a non-guaranteed portfolio, do you fully understand the likely range of returns? What is your worst year likely to be (statistically)? And when it happens (and it will), what will you do?

How much (if any) would you like to leave your children?

How do you wish to handle the cost of custodial care should you need it (and you probably will)?

If you choose to make no changes, what are your chances for success? Are you okay with that?

Step Three: The Consideration--Only after the map is fully drawn can the direction you want to take be determined. Back when Dan's blood results showed he had too much sugar in his blood, he and his doctor together discussed the ups and downs of the strategy: costs, time, denial of certain foods, etc. Once that was outlined, then they created a written plan.

Medications can be used to fight illness. The doctor does not care where you fill the prescription. He simply wants you to take the meds.

In personal finance, products are the medication. While a coach can assist you in acquiring them, it should not be a requirement for being coached. Sadly, we too often see financial advisors offer "free" planning. There is no such thing as free. You will pay for it, one way or another. Typically, the "plan" is nothing more than a sales proposal to buy product. "We'll give you a free plan that will recommend you buy a commission-based product from us."

Working with a fee-based fiduciary advisor you will receive a written plan. We provide you with a list of recommendations on a single page. With each recommendation, we ask a few simple questions:

1. Do you fully understand this recommendation? Do you know the pros and cons?

2. Are you going to implement it (yes or no...never a "let me think about it")?

3. How are you going to implement it? Are you going work with someone (insurance agent, investment advisor)?

4. When are you going to implement it?

No loose ends.

Step Four: The Coaching & Education Stage-- Our firm educates our clients one on one. Each client has unique needs, and they cannot be thrown into one big room and given the same advice. Being a single woman has its own uniqueness and educating you is vital. The financial advisor is the driver going down the road you have mapped out. If I go to fast or slow or make a turn to the left or the right, you need to know why.

Closing Thoughts

Thank you for taking time to read this book. Hopefully, it showed you a new way to view the numerous issues surrounding personal finance and especially women and finance.

If you would like to take the next step to overcome many of the trappings discussed here, do so by calling Dekker Financial Services, LLC or email Meredith.dekker@dekkerfinancial.com_

Mention this book and you will receive 20% off our financial planning fees.

Best regards,

Meredith Dekker ChFC®, CDFA®

www.dekkerfinancial.com